Beyond Beige

A WOMAN'S ILLUSTRATED STORY OF OLD AGE

First published by Ortus Press,
an imprint of Free Association Books
Copyright © 2024 Sylvie Boulay
The authors rights are fully asserted. The rights of
Sylvie Boulay to be identified as the author of this work
has been asserted by her in accordance with the
Copyright, Designs and Patents Act 1988

A CIP Catalogue of this book is available from the British Library

ISBN: 978-1-911-38388-8

Typeset by Typo•glyphix
www.typoglyphix.co.uk

Cover design by Candescent
Illustrations by Sylvie Boulay

Printed and bound in England

To all the other old women

What this book is about

I was born in Paris in 1951. My life until my 60s has been busy and
varied. I moved to Britain, had two marriages and divorces and a lot
of different jobs, homes and interests. The best thing was having
a daughter and then in time a granddaughter. Then things started
to change. Slowly at first with just a few clues here and there. Not
a sudden jump or a fork in the road, more like a gradual change in
the light. I realised I was old and I was living in a different world
from my family and the other young people around me. I could still
operate in their world but I belonged elsewhere.

I live in the world of old women. It can be depressing but it is often very funny. And for some reason, an endless stream of cartoons appears in my mind.

This book is about old women, the joys and the horrors of our old age and all the weird things that happen to us. The experience of ageing may be similar for men but I cannot speak for them. I am not celebrating old age, nor am I complaining about it. It is infinitely preferable to dying young.

I tell my story of ageing exactly as it is, warts and all. This is my experience and also that of women I have watched or spoken to.

I was not sure where to start. Getting old feels like a big clump of compacted odd bits that have rolled and grown over the years and cannot be teased out.

I thought of going through each in turn; the past, present and future but they are all entangled. I did not fancy a timeline because life is too messy and I cannot draw straight lines.

The older I get and the more I feel that my mind and my body are separate. They used to be synchronised and I was unaware of each distinct part of me unless I stubbed my toe or walked into a door. Now different limbs and organs loudly demand my attention. I do not find that a leg suddenly hops off on its own but each part of me is only loosely connected to the rest.

My brain is the worst culprit. It takes over completely or abandons me without warning. So, I decided the best way of starting this book would be to list the main topics that take up space in my head. This is how the chapters are organised.

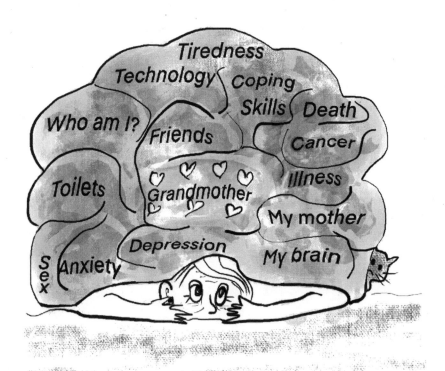

What you will find in this book

Chapter 1

You know you are old when...

You have a paper address book with more dead people than live ones

She should throw it away but she might not remember who is dead

Your eyebrows are migrating South

You remember typewriters and drawing Twiggy eyelashes on your face

Grandma, what are they?

You struggle to stay awake during the day

but you can't sleep at night

You think differently about future savings

(Old) men patronise you

There is more life behind you than in front

Chapter 2

My precious brain

I do not forget anything important; in fact, I probably remember too much. I have yet to go out in my pyjamas but I do not always remember names or the end of a film or why I went into another room. I kid myself that it is because my mind is very busy.

During the menopause, I felt like I was in a dark, crowded attic holding a torch. I could only see what was in the beam and the rest was in shadow. Nowadays the whole place is lit up but it is exhausting to keep looking. My brain fills up too quickly and needs a rest.

Sadly, my brain is still brilliant at conjuring up dark shadows.

My thoughts roll like marbles across a table and fall off somewhere. Sometimes they bounce up again, sometimes they are lost for good. I catch them with pen and paper before they vanish.

Maybe that is a blessing and a fuzzy yesterday brings a clearer today.

On a good day, my brain jumps out of bed before my
sleepy body and starts erupting with ideas.

By mid-morning it starts to float away.

After lunch, my brain wants a rest.

And by afternoon, it's out for the count.

If I am lucky, I can function on autopilot for the rest of the day.

My brain often wakes up
suddenly in the night and
my thoughts somersault
until morning.

Chapter 3

Depression

I find it easier to talk to my female friends about our bodily functions than about depression. It is particularly hard to talk to the ones who have experienced catastrophic loss. How can I possibly ask them if they often feel that they are wading through a dark heaviness?

I struggle to make sense of the depression. It is not just because the time ahead is limited and inevitably worse from a health point of view. Nor because most future joy is likely to be lived through someone else's experience. Nor is it simply because of the extra effort of moving a creaking body.

It is a loneliness which is not abated by being with others.

Sometimes I wonder: is it better if someone is watching even if that someone is not friendly?

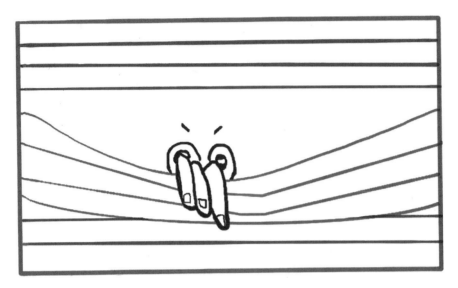

Or is it better if I am on my own?

Changing the setting makes little difference.

It feels like there is a constant war taking place in my brain.

I have become cautious and fearful. Maybe this is what I miss the most, knowing I will never again be as carefree and thoughtless as I once was. At 18 I left Paris with a small suitcase and a big smile, heading for fun and freedom in London. Now I would not dream of running off to start a radically different new life.

Chapter 4

Anxiety

Anxiety and depression are so closely linked in my daily life that I cannot tell where one ends and the other starts.

Fear lurks in the background like a wallpaper.

Doubt has invaded my brain like a virus and I now live in a new age of uncertainty.

Did I lock the door?

Will I be late?

Will my family be OK?

Will I get dementia?

Will I have enough money?

Dr Google says it could be cancer

How long have I got?

What will happen to the planet?

How will I cope?

Everyday problems become matters of survival.

I worry about forgetting something essential but I like to travel light.

I used to think 'that's OK, I'll manage'. Now I focus on possible losses and whether I would cope if something bad happened. Change has always been around but it has become the enemy to be tamed at all costs. I try against all hope to create some certainty: I make lists, I think through every scenario, I carry spares of everything. I avoid danger of any kind. And the fact that I have so far dealt reasonably well with every mishap is not at all reassuring.

Chapter 5

Tiredness

More than grey hair or wrinkles, being so tired is the major change. I can still do almost everything I used to do but I am like an old mobile phone which needs recharging too often.

I strive to be the ideal me but it never lasts.

This new tiredness is nothing like the sleep deprivation of the baby years when all I lusted after was a whole night's sleep. It is not like running on empty when I could still summon enough energy to keep going. It is more like this...

Sitting down, eating or distracting myself does not help. Sometimes I am so tired that I get stuck in my chair.

In the evenings, if I struggle to keep going, I pretend to be a robot and I command her to do my jobs.

Sometimes I can get a bit more energy if I feel angry.

I have yet to curl up in a ball on the pavement but I am often tempted.

I can accept being tired but I cannot bear that I have only a finite amount of energy to get through the day. I should be grateful that it gets replenished every night but it still sucks.

Chapter 6

Illness and cancer

No-one can reach their sixties without having experienced their share of health problems.

After a routine blood test, I discovered I had a rare chronic form of cancer in my bone marrow. It took a long time for the diagnosis to be confirmed and several haematologists had a go at giving me the news.

First there was the gentle but confusing approach.

Then there was the full-frontal approach which I did understand.

I ended up liking this doctor the best because I knew he would tell me the whole truth.

There was also a well-meaning but rather terminal promise from a kind doctor.

I am very lucky that the blood cancer does not affect me very much other than the regular blood tests and hospital visits. The one exception is an absolute terror at the thought of running out of my daily chemo tablets.

A few years later, I noticed a small indentation in my right breast. I was not unduly worried because I had had benign lumps before. I might have waited but my daughter announced she was pregnant, so I got it checked quickly to make sure any treatment needed was finished before the baby arrived. It turned out to be cancer. Again, I was lucky, it was caught early and treatment was manageable.

Sometimes I panic 'Two cancers, when do I get the third one?' and I imagine new cancers everywhere. There are times when I want to escape my body.

I am very grateful that I have lived so long but there is always a risk of misunderstanding life expectancy statistics.

Chapter 7

The toilet diaries

I am talking about incontinence. The list is long: getting up many times in the night, sitting near the exit in cinemas, feeling guilty when I forget my pelvic floor exercises, planning trips around loos... I could be a public toilet critic, except so many have closed down.

Some situations are very tricky.

After years of chronic cystitis, I was prescribed a magical HRT cream. I was told to rub a pea size amount on my urethra.

My body doesn't look anything like the picture on the leaflet.

I know every hack to fully empty my bladder.

Leaning forward

Relaxing

Taking a walk

Thinking of water

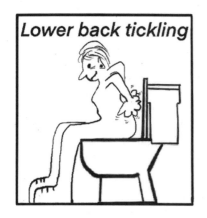

Lower back tickling

Taking my time

Thankfully,
there is
more talk
about
incontinence
these days
but adverts
always
show happy
endings.

My worst fear

Chapter 8

Technology

This is my biggest bugbear. I can mend physical things but technology sends me into whirls of despair. Learning to use my tablet to write this book was a huge challenge.

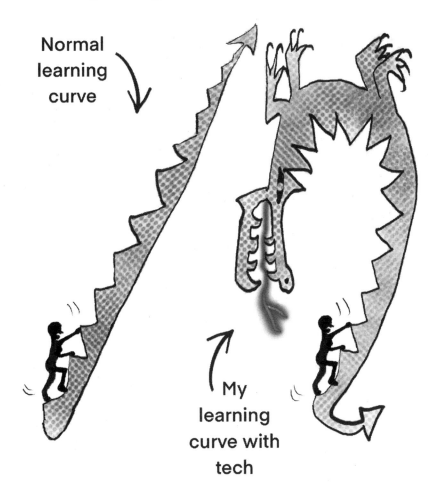

Normal learning curve

My learning curve with tech

Scammers lie in wait for me to try and buy things online so they can ruin me.

It is not just the fear of being hacked and all my information or money stolen. I also hate being dependent on the young people in my life.

I feel I do not belong in a world where everything is done online. If I am bold enough to try and speak to a human being, I am forced to wait hours as a punishment.

If you give me a manual, I will painstakingly work through it. But please do not expect me to pick anything up intuitively. 'It's obvious' says my young expert, 'just do it!' as I return to prehistory.

Chapter 9

Sex

I would rather have a cat on my lap than a lover in my life.

I love the cats running up to sleep with me.

Worries about sex are behind me now. The only creature I share sleeping space with is a persistent cat (or two).

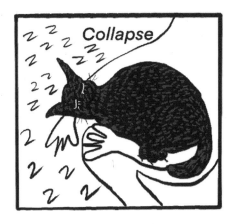

I enjoy the extra space in my brain since I have stopped thinking about sexual relationships. My fantasies have changed over the years.

The old-fashioned French view is that a person does not need to look young but they must look beautiful... (strangely, this does not apply to men!).

When I see happy couples, I sometimes feel sad that I am not one of them. I would like to go as a pair on holiday or to restaurants. But most of the time I am relieved I do not have to fit in with anyone and I love to live on my own. Most of all I relish the fact that I no longer want to be sexually attractive to anyone, although I have not given up on looking as good as I can.

Chapter 10

Grandmothering

This is the very best bit of my old age. I struggled to get pregnant and then my daughter arrived, a one-off miracle. When her own daughter was born, I discovered that the fierce, unique love I felt did indeed expand to enfold another person.

I may not be alive when she becomes an adult so every year with her is infinitely precious. Being involved with her is the greatest of gifts.

It is a huge relief that rules about bedtimes, schools or vaccinations are not mine to make. But I dread every upset and every tumble.

When I am so tired that keeping my face together is an effort, my sweet granddaughter asks:

Do you need a nap?

She sees every wrinkle but she loves my soft stretchy skin. She finds beauty where I do not.

I am the teller of stories about my granddaughter's mother when she was little. I am also the expert at sourcing the best pastries. Her favourite French word is "le goûter" which means after school snack. It would traditionally be plain bread and a few squares of chocolate. She prefers a flan or a pain au chocolat or bread and strong French cheeses. She relishes the delicacies I used to eat as a child but now no longer eat, like frogs' legs and snails. She loves trying new foods.

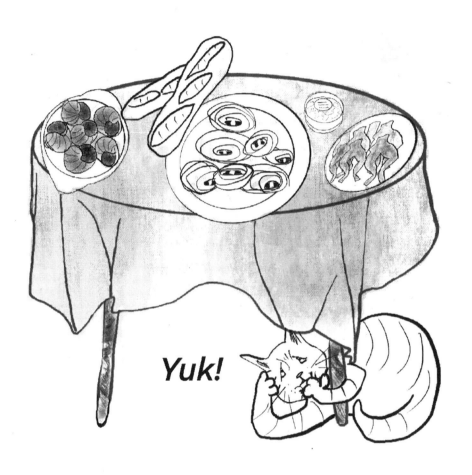

Yuk!

Chapter 11

Friendships

Friendships are different now. When I was young, making friends involved colliding with someone, feeling a bond and moving along on the same path for a while. Friends were fellow students, neighbours, other mums, workmates... and I picked up friendships in a haphazard way as I travelled along. Many lasted and others did not.

Now that I am old, new friendships are more deliberate. The attraction is the same but there is a survival element to my friendships. They are not just about enjoying someone's company; they are also about mutual support.

My new definition of a good friend: someone who tells me when I have a leakproof pad attached to my jeans.

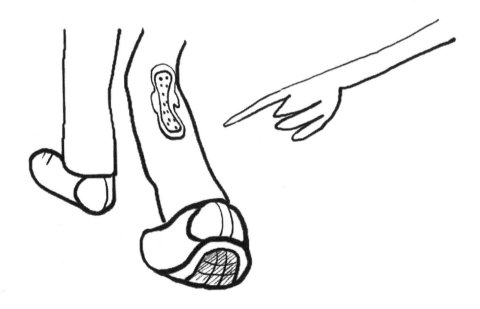

We lie a lot more than before:

We share our respective mental declines.

We share our lack of energy – too tired to walk so we bask in the sun like lizards.

There are pleasant surprises.

And love always shines through.

Chapter 12

Who am I?

Growing up in Paris there were many expectations about how I looked and what I did.

Now I am no longer defined by my looks or by a role or a job. I am automatically slotted into the 'old woman' category and how I look or what I do is almost irrelevant. Occasionally I grieve for my younger self and what she could do. Sometimes I get angry that I am mostly invisible.

It takes longer but I can still transform every morning.

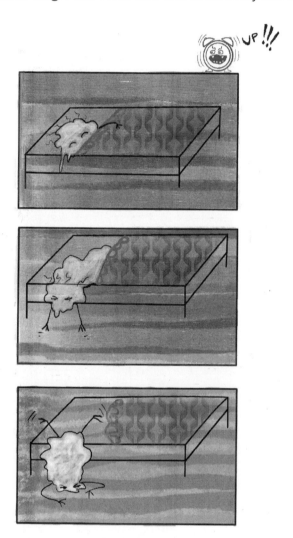

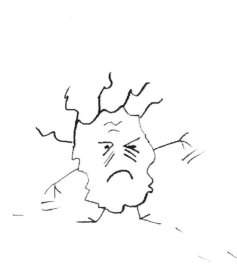
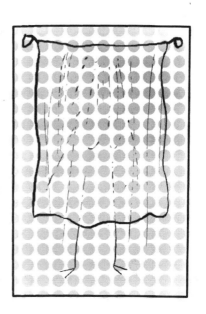

I have faded over the years like an old photo gradually losing its colour. My outline is softer and I have turned grey. Not just my hair or eyebrows, the whole of me is getting paler. Each day I leak a bit more substance.

I noticed it first with the eyes of men in the street skimming past my face. Now men do not see me at all, they even bump into me sometimes.

And then there is the little old lady dilemma: can I pick and choose when it suits me to be old and frail?

Nowhere is this more evident than on public transport. Do I accept a seat when it is offered? If I refuse, the kind person may never offer their seat again, so I am doing a disservice to old people everywhere. If I take the seat, I instantly age another 10 years. Either way, the person who offered will avoid all eye contact with me for the rest of the journey.

Do I insist on sitting upstairs on buses and creep like a crab on my way down or do I plonk myself with a sigh in the seats reserved for old people?

Most of the time I manage to ignore what anyone thinks about me or what I am.

Sadly, this is often what happens when old women dare to stick their heads above the parapet...

But on the other hand…

Chapter 13

My mother

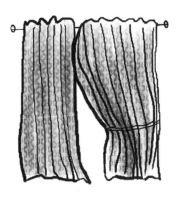

I grew up in a traditional block of flats in the 9th arrondissement which was then a rundown part of Paris. My father lived there all his life and his family had chosen it because it faced north and the sun would not damage their furnishings.

It took years before my parents had basic amenities like running hot water. We boiled water on a hob and each had our own plastic bowl to wash in. My parents only installed a bathroom after I left home following a visit to England where they enjoyed the sanitation. I do not remember smelling bad.

When I was small my mother would take me to a local bathhouse. I loved the enormous bath, the thick towels and the tiny bars of perfumed soap. I was frightened of the drain which I suspected might swallow me up with the bath water.

Food was very important. We had the typical French three meals a day and there was the occasional ordeal of having to eat foods that made me gag like raw minced steak and shellfish. My parents could not accept that I also disliked wine.

I relished the trips to the Rue Lepic market where butter was cut with a thin wire and greengrocers offered pieces of fruit to try before buying.

It was a difficult time because my parents hated each other. My mother was bright, flamboyant but cold. She was entirely devoid of empathy and enjoyed telling tall tales and playing cruel games.

My mother fell out with her father for several years. When he died, she became severely depressed and eventually psychotic. My own father could not cope and my brother escaped as best he could. Later he was unable to remember a large part of his childhood.

I navigated my way in and out of my mother's delusions. We lived in a flat with rooms arranged on either side of a corridor. For months, she was convinced that a railway line ran along the corridor. To keep her calm, I dutifully checked for passing trains before moving from one room to another.

She regularly tried to kill herself by climbing out of the window of our 4th floor flat. The bedroom doors had metal handles shaped like mermaids. Fortunately, they creaked loudly so I always had time to run and pull her back.

Her psychiatrist gave her medication which stopped all this but turned her into a zombie for a while which was much more frightening than the delusions.

She lived a long life after that. I left Paris for London the day after I got the result of my Baccalauréat. She continued to try and control me from a distance.

One of the advantages of growing old is that we can reflect on difficult things in the past and see the positives in what felt utterly miserable at the time. It has taken a very long time but I can now appreciate the extraordinary skills I learned in order to cope. I learned to read a face and to know when I was safe. I learned vigilance. Best of all, I learned to escape and when I could not, to withdraw into some inner space.

Chapter 14

Coping mechanisms

The best bit about being old is that we have irrefutable proof that we have coped so far.

I worked as a counsellor and I continue to use my cognitive therapy training to deal with difficult situations. My first instinct is to reach for pen and paper and list my feelings, my thoughts, the evidence for and the evidence against.

I like to ask myself what is the worst that can happen but that often backfires and I terrify myself.

I wait for it to pass.

I tell myself I will thrive even if I have to turn into a mushroom.

I was bought up a Catholic so I tend to wait for a saviour.

I search for the missing silver lining.

Walking, running and moving generally is what helps me the most.

Chapter 15

Death

I have been terrified of death in the past when it has seemed a very real possibility. I still have a constant fear of other people's death but not of my own. I do worry about pain or being dependent on others. But on a good day, death feels like a proper ending to a good book.

I get stressed about leaving a mess for my family to clear so I declutter regularly.

Many hours later…

There will be the advantage of having no more jobs to do.

I would like to meet all the other possible versions of me that I could have been.

Chapter 16
Last words

To become an old woman, I have survived a lot of regrets, disappointments and loss

but the end of the story is still largely for me to draw.

Despite the depression, the loneliness, the incontinence and the painful joints, there is much to say for old age.

Time is whizzing by now but I enjoy the good bits more than before. I have been lucky that so many fears did not materialise and so much did work out.

There is joy in counting all the things that I no longer have to deal with...

and I feel today's pleasures more keenly.

The 'beige' tyranny...

is well and truly behind me.

There is a newfound (slight) ability to make friends with the unknown

a new degree of freedom to do whatever I want...

and pride at being an old woman.

Acknowledgements

I was brought up on a diet of French comics called Spirou and Tintin. Later I fell in love with Sempé and Brétécher. I never wanted to be an astronaut or a film star, I just dreamed of drawing cartoons.

As I got older and friends shared their stories of ageing, cartoon ideas kept on coming and I just had to sketch them. They were and still are, much better in my head than in real life. Paula Cocozza from the Guardian interviewed me for her 'New life after 60' column and encouraged me to keep going. Alice Solomons, the publishing director of Free Association Books, liked my first draft and told me not to worry too much about the drawings and just get on with it.

I am very grateful to all the people who made this book possible with their ideas, support and encouragement as well as much needed practical help with technology.

Thank you first to my family, Dee, David and Lyra and their two ever present cats.

Thank you to Alice Solomons who was willing to depart from the usual Free Association Books.

Thank you to a very talented young artist, Sabina ('Godka') Godalyova who gave me cartooning lessons and generously shared her knowledge and skills with infinite patience for more than a year.

Thank you to all the friends who gave me their time and feedback: Denise Riley, Carole Hodson, Lynn and Peter Burke, Miriam Harris, Leah and Tom Wells, Bernadette Boyde and Daphne Romney.

Lastly, thank you to all the women I met over the years who were willing to share their stories.